Introduction by W. Terrence Gordon

Published originally in *The Humanities Association Bulletin* (1961), this essay provides one of the richest commentaries on educational reform to be found anywhere in McLuhan's writings. His programmatic call to action summons the distilled wisdom of management studies visionary Peter Drucker, Bertrand Russell, A. N. Whitehead, Leonardo da Vinci, Harold Innis, and Teilhard de Chardin, a mix that ensures a balanced new perspective for overhauling the study of the humanities. Central ideas from *Understanding Media* are evident here in advanced stages of gestation: the definition of media as outer senses, the subtle assimilation of media of commercial production to language as a medium for the externalization and exchange of the products of thought and experience, the "globally dilated senses" of mankind in the electronic age. And a whimsical McLuhan asserts that "Madison Avenue is the Archimedes of our time," scripting the ancient scientist's time travel to the electronic age with the opening line: "Well, I'll be fulcrummed." — WTG

The Humanities in the Electronic Age

It was Peter Drucker, former professor of philosophy, and now Dean of the School of Management of New York University, who said in effect at the outset of his *Landmarks of Tomorrow*: For the first time in human history higher education is not a privilege, a frill or a luxury; it is a necessity of production. This is not to say that higher education is being supplanted by commerce, but rather that the age-old gap between them is harder to find. In a recent book, *Classrooms in the Factories*, Clark and Sloan report that the annual budget for classroom teaching in industry is more than four times the annual budget for primary, secondary, and higher education. And that estimate takes no account of the extensive management training programmes for military personnel. The G.E. management center for executive training at Crotonville on the Hudson has four classes of forty executives each year. The budget is 46 million. Never did he know the true meaning of liberal education, says Peter Drucker in the book already mentioned, until he entered the field of management consulting. He refers to the immediate relevance of encyclopedic liberal knowledge in the conduct of current corporation design and action. Indeed, the corporations are much more aware of their need for high-level liberal education than are the universities. The Ciceronian ideal of the *doctus orator* is current again. In *The Liberal Hour*, Kenneth Galbraith has a chapter on "Economics and Art," in which he both ridicules the old commercial notion of arts as frivolity and urges the relevance of art as navigational guide in all business today. The supremacy of design in creating and markets is one factor. The other factor is that the artist's designs provide the advance models of future development. The old-fashioned business man who played it off the cuff and read only the current signs is now doomed by the speed of the new technology. So the artist moves from the Ivory Tower to the Control Tower in modern industry.

With regard to the new needs of industry in the electronic age a recent spokesman insisted that one out of every ten elementary school children must proceed to a Ph.D. if the American situation is to be maintained. No matter what the area of study be, so it be done in depth, that is the vision of American business in education today, for good or ill.

On all hands today it is plain that actualities are much in advance of our thought and theory. When everything changes at once because everything has become inter-dependent, we can expect from the very heart of change a plangent cry for permanence and stability. A second-grade teacher, just after Sputnik, asked her class to write poems about the event. She was quite amazed at the results and showed them to me. One of them I wrote down. It went:

The stars are so big
The moon is so small
Stay as you are.

That, whether verbalized or not, is the message and the logic, not of the mechanical age just past, but of the electronic age in which we stand as primitives of an underdeveloped and unknown culture. Those of us who have had special regard for the ancient disciplines that passed out of our schools years ago will see them return and flourish as never before. The generations immediately ahead of us will scorn the recent decades and even centuries as periods of triviality, frivolity, and of planned obsolescence. We shall see all communities, as well as all commodities and dwellings, assume a stubborn, depth character of organic persistence, as if built by Frank Lloyd Wright. Survey programmes will disappear from the curricula of studies as the panic for permanence drives us into ever greater depth understanding of all kinds of knowledge and action.

I say this without enthusiasm. It is not exhilarating to foresee the inexorable discovery of one's own childish ways of thought. Many a teenager today in his passionate pursuit of a crash programme in adulthood looks on parent and teacher alike as superficial and banal in their modes of routinized living. The situation is the same on the non-personal level. We are all familiar with the computation based on a survey of present-day scientific development: that of all the greatest scientists who ever lived, 95 percent are living right now. Does this mean that there is more human intelligence now than before? Not at all. But it does mean that we have hit upon some means of activating intelligence that is new. A. N. Whitehead pointed to the discovery of the nineteenth century as the discovery of the technique of invention. Bertrand Russell pointed to the the great achievement of the twentieth century as the technique of suspended judgement. That is, the discovery of the process of insight itself, the technique of avoiding the automatic closure of involuntary fixing of attitudes that so easily results from any given cultural situation. The technique of open field perception. Both the discovery of the method of invention and the discovery of the technique of insight not only concern scientists but humanists, and have been freely used by both of what C.P. Snow calls the two cultures. So much so, indeed, that the resonant statistic of about 95 percent of the greatest scientists of human history now being alive may apply equally to poets, painters, and philosophers. Perhaps we in this group ought really to ask ourselves why we tend instinctively to reject the idea that we might be living in the greatest of all intellectual and artistic periods, even though we may endorse the ebullient scientific estimate of our time. At any period of the past, humanists have been distinguished by a love of ruins and by a gloomy sense that change and decay invest the scene. Perhaps Lord Macaulay hit upon a new strategy. Convinced that he did not live in the greatest of all human centuries, he compensated for his non-humanist buoyancy by giving us the memorable image of the New Zealander who would one day arrive to sit upon a fragment of London Bridge in order to sketch the ruins of St. Paul's. Petrarch in a famous passage which has often been misread as a glorious prophecy of the great Renaissance so near to him, actually stood amidst the ruins of Rome and stated that just as assuredly as there had been uninterrupted decline from Augustan days to his own time, so in the years that lay ahead there would be continuous decay of such classical treasures and skills as still remained. Gibbon was faithful to the same perspective when he tells us in his *Autobiography*:

> It was at Rome on the fifteenth of October, 1764, as I sat musing amidst the ruins of the Capitol, while the barefooted friars were singing Vespers, in the temple of Jupiter, that the idea of writing the decline and fall of the city first started to my mind.

May I suggest a face-saving device in this humanist obsession with ruins and decay? The humanist is a Luddite, as C. P. Snow calls him, because he gets a thrill of imagined potential from the fragmentary, and tends to feel that the complete structure offers no mode of creative empathy or participation. Thus the humanist is more fascinated by the incomplete *Hyperion* of Keats than by the complete *Prelude* of Wordsworth.

It has been said that had Milton broken off his *Paradise Lost* at the end of the fourth book, his reputation would stand above any poet of antiquity. The fragment we possess of the *Faerie Queene*, perhaps spurs more speculation than would a completed twenty-four-book structure. Let me return a moment to the observation of A. N. Whitehead's, that the great discovery of the nineteenth century was the discovery of the technique of discovery. At least in *Science in the Modern World*, where he makes this statement, Whitehead does not explain his point. Edgar Allan Poe, whom Baudelaire and Valery regarded as the nineteenth-century Leonardo da Vinci, did explain the point in his "Philosophy of Composition." The technique of invention is to begin with the *effect* one wishes to achieve and then to go *backwards* to the point from which to begin to produce that effect, and only that effect. In a sense this technique of starting with the effect, before seeking the causes and means of the effect, is the perfection of the assembly-line method. It is a method of organized ignorance. Because, whether one wishes to make a car or a poem, a guided missile or a detective story, it is necessary to begin with the solution or effect. Dickens found that writing for serial publication compelled him to plan ahead. And assembly-line methods imply complete analysis and total reconstruction backwards from the end-product. This power of advance segmental analysis of each phase of a complex operation was bequeathed to us by Gutenberg and his moveable types. It is a technique made obsolete by electrically recorded tapes. The assembly-line yields now to galaxy clusters of simultaneous operations which are made possible by the exact synchronization of the information on tapes. The humanist will observe, however, that no matter what period or technology is in question, the artist has always solved the new problem both for the engineer and for the human community, by his new advance models for sensibility and awareness. The exact models of coming forms provided by artistic intuition are like "the providence that's in a watchful state," which, as Ulysses says to Achilles in Shakespeare's *Troilus and Cressida*,

Knows almost every grain of Plutus' gold,
Finds bottom in the uncomprehensive deeps,
Keeps place with thought, and almost like the gods
Does thoughts unveil in their dumb cradles.

The ever new models of the artist are for the correction of the perceptual bias inflicted upon any human community by ever new technology. In the past century, indeed, we have come to rely almost wholly on art for the nutrition of fresh impulse and the alerting of hypnotized senses. No previous society ever regarded art this way. But no previous society ever underwent the successive brain-washings and hypnotic trances that ours has done from a succession of new technologies.

Now to come to the Bertrand Russell point — that the great discovery of the twentieth century concerns the technique of the suspended judgement. The technique of insight itself is a natural phase to succeed the nineteenth-century discovery of the technique of invention, because it is the means of abstracting oneself from the bias and consequences of one's own culture. If a merely negative criterion were needed it would be easy to infer from the dismay and incomprehension which the later work of Harold Innis has caused in the minds of his admirers that he had finally hit upon a discovery of a very considerable and a very exacting nature.

Innis' concern in *The Bias of Communication*, and later, is with the technique of the suspended judgement. That means, not the willingness to admit other points of view, but the technique of how not to have a point of view. This is identical with the problem facing physicists in correcting the bias of the instruments of research, and it draws attention to the fact that the historian, the poet, the critic, and the philosopher, now as always, face exactly the same situations as the scientist. This is easy to see in larger historical retrospect. Failure to see it in the present may be the results of what Galbraith calls "vested interests in acquired knowledge" of involvement or anxiety or stupefaction or fatigue. But there are now some quite new factors in the over-all situation which need to be specified. Whatever may prove to be the weaknesses of Teilhard de Chardin's work, he will always have the credit of having correctly defined the major change of our age. In *The Phenomenon of Man* he observes:

> It has been stated over and over again. Through the discovery yesterday of the railway, the motor car and the airplane, the physical influence of each man, formerly restricted to a few miles, now extends to hundreds of leagues or more. Better still, thanks to the prodigious biological event represented by the discovery of electro-magnetic waves, each individual finds himself henceforth (actively and passively) simultaneously present, over land and sea, in every corner of the earth.

The end of mechanism, the extension of organic interdependence to every phase of experience and human association is what has happened to us. Behind us are the twenty-five or more centuries during which the Western world perfected the means of moving the *products* of human discourse and human ingenuity to every corner of the earth. This was done mainly by the alphabet and print and their derivatives in transport and industry. By abstracting sight and sound, by arresting the movements of speech and thought into a visual code, we extended the techniques of mechanical analysis and packaging to the whole of human discourse and learning.

But what has happened with the electronic advent is not that we move the products of human knowledge or labour to all corners of the earth more quickly. Rather we dilate the very means and *processes* of discourse to make a global envelope of sense and sensibility for the earth. From the moment of the telegraph, extrasensory perception became a daily factor in shaping the human community and private perception alike. It is not the products of perception and judgement which now reach us by electric media, but involvement in the entire communal process of interfused coexistence. Each one of us, actively or passively, includes every other person on earth. The world no longer offers the possibility of the separatist, center-margin structure which is featured in all our institutions, legal, educational, political. Centres-without-margins, inclusive consciousness, inclusive organization, these alone are viable or relevant to the new electric age. One can readily sympathize with a ferocious intellectual Luddite like Jacques Barzun, who in an inclusive negation of our new age, says: "Away with Art, Science, and Philanthropy." He finds all three so monstrously demanding and possessive that he is probably right in concluding that the free-wheeling days of solitary *laissez-faire* are finished, and the House of Intellect must be builded anew and by other means.

The sheer dilation of sight and sound and touch and movement to encompass the earth is entirely consistent with Bertrand Russell's point that the great discovery of the twentieth century is the technique of suspended judgement. For as our private senses now go beyond us to the ends of the earth, as our wits go out of us, it becomes necessary for us to develop a consensus among our outer senses or media. And the pressure towards this consensus has given us a clairvoyance about the *process* of human awareness which we might call insight. Even now we continue to act a good deal as if our outer senses, the electronic media, were still private. Archimedes had rightly observed; "Give me a place to stand and I will move the word." Today, looking at our globally dilated senses, he would comment: "Well, I'll be fulcrummed. Why I can stand on your ear, on your eye, on your skin and move the world as I wish."

Up until the advent of electro-magnetism the Western world had merely externalized and exchanged the products of thought and experience. We are quite unprepared for the much higher educational demands of the present situation in which we must share the actual processes of thought and experience of all mankind. But this new necessity not only compels us to inspect our own processes of thought and perception more carefully than in any previous age, but it urges us to the most earnest inquiry into all past art, literature and culture in order to benefit from all past discoveries about the processes of insight. The humanities are moving out of their centuries-old consumer and appreciation phase into a depth phase of rigorous producer-orientation. Instead of merely establishing a perspective for past cultures, our tendency today is to reconstruct entire past cultures from within. A whole galaxy of procedures is available to this end. But the result is very different from the perspective and views of the past that became possible at the Renaissance. Instead of a fine background and foreground, with central and peripheral organization, the total reconstruction procedure is less visual than empathic. It is a structure of simultaneous and organic inter-relationships.

This change of structure resulting from new means of information is of the greatest relevance in understanding the changed situation of the humanities today. We have in the past century moved out of a mechanical into an electric, organic culture. That is, we have increasingly moved out of a segmental, specialist phase of knowledge into a period of interplay and, as it were, dialogue among all kinds of knowledge. And, whereas the mechanical age had been one of center-margin structures, the electronic age is inevitably one of multiple centres-without-margins. Under conditions of simultaneity of access to information, Cuba is not a margin politically, nor is Laos. They are centres as much as London or Moscow or Washington, yet our assumptions are still otherwise. Hence our confusion.

In the world of Top Management, the same confusion reigns. More development has occurred in the past decade in management, say the leading consultants, than in the previous fifty years. And the change is all decentralist. Delegated authority simply won't work under conditions of electric information movement. Instead, only the "authority knowledge" will work. And this means that a manager today has to know the over-all operation.

Today, one of the most interesting developments in American education concerns the new honours programmes for the top students. This programme is steering away from the old centre-margin pattern of lectures towards the inclusive centre-without-margin pattern of the tutorial.

Another major upset in centre-margin patterns of education concerns the idea of university extension. Just as business is discovering that higher and higher education is needed for the ever enlarging jobs of management, so the adult community in general has become aware of the life of learning as natural and delightful and as necessarily extended throughout adult life.

Another way of getting at this in terms of the humanities in the Electronic Age is to reflect on the fact that A. T. & T., by far the largest business in the world, with a gross national product equal to that of the entire Canadian economy, does nothing but move information. No wheels, no shafts, no belts, just the movement of information. The coding and moving and use of information will soon be the main business of all mankind. And as the work force withdraws from its present industrial occupations, with the aid of automation, learning will be the paid occupation of all mankind from infancy onward. The entire globe will be a single campus, for such in large measure it is at the present hour.

Our existing ideas of educational organization are still of the centre-margin pattern of institutionalized structure that is taken for granted by the baffled administrator as he meditates on the explosion in student population and the explosion in learning. How is this centre-margin pattern to be maintained *and* TV fitted into it? How is the entire community to receive a higher education *and* present standards of instruction to be maintained? The answer is simple and it has been rendered many times by other new structures in the electronic age: decentralize. Create multiple new centres. Abandon centre-margin patterns of the old hierarchy of specialties and functions. Enthrone the living dialogue in centres and between centres, since the entire new technology of our age demands this greatest of all humanist forms of instruction, not as an ideal, but as a daily necessity of action in every area of our communities.

The humanities, then, are about to enter their greatest period of cultivation and expression in the electronic age. But they will assume different relations to each other than we have latterly known them to have. In the ancient world and in the medieval period the trivial and quadrivial studies were, in the main, centres without margins. They are returning as such, but where they were seven before, they may soon be seventy. And there will be no more incompatibility of the *Two Cultures* that C. P. Snow has reminded us of. The real trouble has been that the literary and verbal culture has followed the nineteenth-century logic of mechanism and specialism just as far as the scientists have followed the merely statistical logic of numbers. With the computer all move out of the age of number and statistics into the age of the curve and the simultaneous awareness of structures. With satellite broadcasting a few months off, we move, scientist and humanist alike, into the world of instant and inexpensive access to anything and anybody on the globe. The divorce in our world is not now, nor will it be, between the scientist and the humanist but between the mechanist and the electrician. Our scientists as much as our humanists are caught in the old forms of the departing mechanical culture which all have contributed to for centuries. We now live electrically, but we continue to think in the older modes of mechanism. Even the wheel itself, which we abstracted from animal form, is being reabsorbed into the organic in the jet age. In the Polaris missile the fuel and the engine are one. Both cease to exist at the same moment. Yet the mark of obsolescence is now, as always, hypertrophy. Witness the motor car.

When he set out to give us his *ABC of Relativity*, Bertrand Russell explained:

> Many of the ideas can be expressed in non-mathematical language, but they are none the less difficult on that account. What is demanded is a change in our imaginative picture of the world . . . The same sort of change was demanded by Copernicus when he taught that the earth is not stationary and the heavens do not revolve about it once a day. To us now there is no difficulty in this idea because we learned it before our mental habits had become fixed. Einstein's ideas, similarly, will seem easier to generations which grow up with them; but for us a certain effort of imaginative reconstruction is unavoidable.

One major difference between the age of Copernicus and that of Einstein is the fact that there was nobody who could apply the ideas of Copernicus to anything but poetry and painting. Today the most abstruse theories go into action even before they have had their day in science fiction.

Yet today, as never before, the task of the humanities is to keep clear and lively the modes of discourse and the forms of mental life. More than ever before humanists are called on to understand many new languages born of the new forms of new knowledge. Nor will these new languages obviate the older ones. Jet travel and satellite broadcasting will foster the grasp of languages, ancient and modern, in a simultaneous cultural transparency. The concept of history of the philosopher Heidegger recommends itself as a natural model for the humanities in the electric age. It is the idea of the poetic of history, of history as a kind of unified language, the inner key to the creation of which can be grasped by a deepening sense of the spiritual energy encompassed in the ceaselessly growing life of words. The ideal Marriage of Mercury and Philology, of spiritual values and perfected method, will be consummated, if ever, in the electronic age.

The Humanities in the Electronic Age
Marshall McLuhan - Unbound (07)

ISBN: 1-58423-051-7
Library of Congress Control Number 2005927213

Marshall McLuhan Unbound Project Editors
Eric McLuhan, W. Terrence Gordon

Published in United States in October 2005 by
Gingko Press, Inc.
5768 Paradise Drive, Suite J · Corte Madera, CA 94925
(415) 924-9615 · Fax (415) 924-9608
email: books@gingkopress.com
http://www.gingkopress.com

Design, packaging and production: Die Gestalten Verlag, Berlin
Layout and Typography: onlab, Berlin
Fonts: *Dolly* by Underware, *Bullet* by House Industries
Production: Martin Bretschneider, Vinzenz Geppert
Art direction: Robert Klanten

Made in Germany